W9-BJD-755

Swedish Proverbs

"Fair flowers don't remain long by the wayside."

Collected by Joanne Asala

For Bill Orejudos. "It is never too far to a friend's house."

Acknowledgments

A special thank-you to Tom Blanck, St. Paul, Minnesota, for use of his historic collection of Swedish books; Dr. John Lofgren, former director of the American Swedish Institute in Minneapolis, Minnesota, for assistance with the manuscript; Kerstin Olsson Van Gilder, Mary Lou Hattery, and Dean and Charlotte Anderson. Editorial Staff: Dorothy Crum and John Zug. Design: Robyn B. Loughran.

Front Cover: Baltic Islands near Stockholm. Back Cover: Midsummer Churchboat in Dalarna. Photographs ©1994 Joan Liffring-Zug. Illustrations in this book are from *Svenska Turist-Föreningens Årsskrift* by Ezaline Boheman. Published by Wahlström and Widstrand. Stockholm, 1906 and 1913.

Select List of Consulted Sources and Recommended Reading

Arnfeldt, Arvid. *Winged Words*. Stockholm, ca. 1890.
Bechtel, John H. *Proverbs, Maxims and Phrases Drawn from Many Lands*. London, 1906.
Christy, Robert. *Proverbs Maxims and Phrases*. New York, 1887.
Conklin, George. *The World's Best Proverbs*. Philadelphia, 1906.
Dennys, E.M. *Proverbs and Quotations of Many Lands*. London, 1890.
Hood, E.P. *The World of Proverb and Parable*. London, 1885.
Hulme, F. Edward. *Proverb Lore*. London: Elliot Stock, 1902.
Johnson, H. *Proverbs*. New York, 1885.
Kelly, Walter K. *Proverbs of All Nations*. London, 1859.
Kelly, Walter K. *A Collection of the Proverbs of All Nations*. Andover, 1879.
King, W. F. H. *Classical and Foreign Quotations*. London, 1889.
Marvin, D. E. *Curiosities in Proverbs*. London, 1916.
Mayo. *Stories and Sayings of Europe*. London, 1912.
Middlemore, James. *Proverbs, Sayings and Comparisons in Various Languages*. London, 1889.
O'Leary, C.F. *The World's Best Proverbs and Proverbial Phrases*. St. Louis, 1907.
Renterdahl, H. *Old Proverbs from the Swedish*. 1840.
Renterdahl, H. *Swedish Book of Proverbs*. 1865.
Shearer, William. *Wisdom of the World in Proverbs*. New York, 1904.

The Penfield Press Proverb Series

$10.95 each, postpaid to one address. 1994 prices subject to change.

Swedish Proverbs (this book)	*Scandinavian Proverbs*
Danish Proverbs	*Finnish Proverbs*
Norwegian Proverbs	*Words of Wisdom from the Vikings*

For a complete catalog of titles send $2.00 to:
Penfield Press, 215 Brown Street, Iowa City, Iowa 52245
Copyright ©1994 Joanne Asala
ISBN: 0-941016-98-6   Library of Congress #94-065663

Table of Contents

·VÄTTERN·I·MORGONSTÄMNING·

Introduction

If you want to know a people, study their proverbs. Sweden's rich literary heritage is full of homespun philosophy, simple truths, bits of collective wisdom, and good old common sense. Scholars define a proverb as "a short, wise saying used for a long time by many people." The Swedes put it another way, "a proverb says what all men think."

The Swedish people love beauty, and even their most practical, everyday items are works of art. So, too, are their proverbs. I was delighted to rediscover many of the same words of wisdom that were spoken by my great-grandparents, immigrants from the western regions of Finland.

So enjoy these short, pithy statements from a centuries-old culture, and perhaps you will find that the wisdom of our ancestors still speaks to us today.

About the Author

Joanne Asala is the owner of Kalevala Books, a company that publishes folklore and fairy tale collections. Of Finnish and Polish descent, she grew up in Bloomingdale, Illinois, a suburb of Chicago, and graduated from the University of Iowa, where she studied medieval literature and languages.

Joanne has collaborated with her cousin, Jason Asala, on a children's version of the Middle English ballad *Sir Gawain and the Green Knight,* and has edited a collection of Celtic folktales called *Whistling Jigs to the Moon: Tales of Irish and Scottish Pipers.* Her titles for Penfield Press include *Norwegian Proverbs, Polish Proverbs, Words of Wisdom from the Vikings, Fairy Tales of the Slav Peasants and Herdsmen,* and *Trolls Remembering Norway*—a compilation of stories and essays of trolls in the United States and Norway. She is the editor of several collections of student poetry, including *The Ugly Caterpillar* and *Shadows in the Snow.*

ove and Marriage

Love is a dew that falls
on both nettles
and lilies.

Midsummer night is not long, but
it sets many cradles rocking.

A life without love is like a year
without summer.

A man is often
    too young for marriage,
    but a man is never
        too old to love.

He who cannot
kindle a fire
cannot love.

No thief steals love,
    but love often makes thieves.

Wedlock is like an eel basket.
    Those who are out want to
    get in, and those who are in
    want to get out.

It is well to seek a wife in the
    village, but not in the street.

No one can live on beauty, but
one can die for it.

Love often creeps where it
should not grow.

Love has made heroes of many
and fools of many more.

Love is a flower
which at marriage
bears fruit.

The married man has many cares,
the bachelor many more.

A man without a wife is like a
man without conviction.

A man without a wife is
a man without thought.

Bachelors grow foolish.

Beauty without virtue
is like a rose
without scent.

 isdom and Folly

We all have a fool
    beneath our clothes,
    but some hide it
        better than others.

Empty barrels
    make the loudest rattle.

One gains wisdom
        through suffering.

Unnecessary wisdom is
twofold foolishness.

One finds many
gray hairs but
few wise men.

A wise man has his tongue
in his heart.

It is better to be a fool
than to make
another person
feel foolish.

The wise man is
only cheated once.

Wisdom without use is like
fire without warmth.

If a fool could
keep silent,
he would not
be a fool.

Philosophy and Religion

VRETA · KLOSTERKYRKA

A quiet word stills anger.

Trust in God makes
the nation strong.

Blessed is he
who knows how
to forgive.

The rope has never been made
that can bind thought.

A clear conscience is
the best pillow.

In calm seas
every ship has a
good captain.

All beginnings are difficult.

Praise counsel when you have
heeded it, and ale when
you have drunk it.

The rich man rides and
the poor man goes on foot,
but both reach
Judgment Day
equally fast.

The greater
      the need,
   the nearer
         the Lord is.

Everyone has
      his own devil,
         and some have two.

In a little house
      the Lord has a corner,
in a big house
      He stands in the hall.

Dust is still dust, no matter
 how near to Heaven
   it is blown.

One is either
  a friend of our Lord
    or an enemy.

Man seeks to reach the Lord,
  gold seeks to reach the soul.

When our Lord gives,
  one should keep
    the sack open.

The Lord often
  goes about in
    worn-down shoes.

The Lord gives
every bird its food,
but He does not
cast it into the nest.

own on the Farm

Don't throw away
      the old bucket
      until you know whether
      the new one
      will hold water.

A lazy man raises poor cabbage.

He who cannot carry the stone
      must roll it.

Not all Autumns fill granaries.

When can a lazy man work?
    In Fall there is
        too much mud.
    In Spring there is
        too much water.
    In Winter
        the cold is biting.
    In Summer
        the heat burns.

The work praises the man.

In Spring the
    farmer carries
    a bag of ignorance,
in Autumn
    a bag of wisdom.

By doing nothing
       we learn to do ill.

The clock must be
       master of the house.

A short man gets a strawberry
       from the earth quicker than
       a tall man a star from
       the heavens.

Weeds grow best
       in good soil.

New brooms sweep best.

A good pig
    will find its way
        home at night.

The little pigs
       would grunt in fear
    if they knew the suffering
      of the boar.

Even a blind hen
    will sometimes
        find a grain.

Everyone jumps
      over a low fence.

·TALLBEVUXEN·SANDÅS·

If one sheep bleats,
the whole barnyard
is thirsty.

Give the servant
good food and
the cows will
yield more milk
and the cat will
drink less.

Nature, Day and Night

Even the smallest
of stars shines
in the darkness.

Don't believe the tears
of the ocean, for its eyes
are always full of water.

Day gives
      and night takes.

No one is
      too poor
            to help another,
      and no one is
      too rich never
            to need help.

What the waterfall brings,
      the stream takes away.

A tall tree bends,
      but it does not break.

Water goes where
      water has been.

There is no night so long
that a day
will not follow it.

A rotting tree leans
long before it falls.

One who mocks a stream
should stand by the sea.

One bird in the hand is better
than two on the roof.

He who has taken
    the bear into the boat
    must cross over with him.

The afternoon knows
    what the morning
        never dreamed.

He on whom the sun shines
    asks not about the moon.

One good day often costs a
    hundred bad nights.

The evening is
    the crown of
        the day.

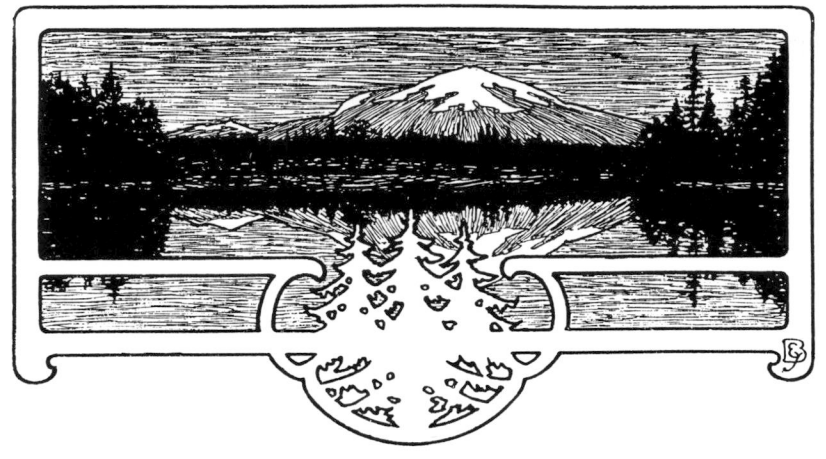

The light shines for others and
    not for itself.

The day we fear
    hurries toward us,
    the day we long for creeps.

That which is
    to become a nettle
        must learn
            to sting early.

A narrow river
is soon rowed,
a shallow ocean
measured,
a small mind
stirred.

Truth
and Lies

If lies were as heavy
   as stones to carry,
many would speak
   only the truth.

Mistakes of others
   make no law.

The greatest right is often
the greatest wrong.

Better to suffer
        for the truth
than be praised
        for the lie.

Eat only
        what is ripe,
speak only
        what is true.

If every lie were to
        knock out a tooth,
there would be many
        toothless people.

The Change of Seasons

What is hidden
in snow
comes forth
in the thaw.

One swallow does not
make Summer.

No one thinks of the snow
that fell last year.

Warm days
in Winter
are still cold.
Cold days
in Summer
are still warm.

The Winter
does not pass
without looking
behind.

He who lies idle
 when the wind is mild,
must row when the wind
 blows against him.

Earth in Spring is worth more than grass in Autumn.

Historic Proverbs

It will not do to go
berry-picking with
the nobleman;
he will keep both berries
and baskets.

When the cat is away,
the rats will dance
on the table.

VADSTENA SLOTT FRÅN LANDSIDAN

Lords without virtue
are like lanterns
without light.

Money travels along
the high road.

In war it is better to
fasten one's horse
to someone else's manger.

What is gained in war
is eaten in war.

Better coarse cloth
than bare thighs.

He who would
harvest honey
must endure the
sting of the bees.

A piece of bread in one's pocket
is better than a
feather in one's hat.

Neither hat nor crown
ever held up
against a
headache.

He who eats his bread
  in solitude,
  saddles his horse
            alone.

The mill goes
      with the current
  and the old woman
          against it.

When the cat
      and mouse agree,
  the farmer's in trouble.

A poor woman has
  many troubles:
      crying babies, wet firewood,
      leaking kettle, and
      a grumpy husband.

LAPSK · TORFKÅTA · VID · HÄLINGEN

In war
all suffer defeat,
even victors.

War makes thieves
and peace hangs them.

The rooster often crows
without a victory.

A man is needed for a day,
a dog for a week,
and a woman always.

riends and Neighbors

No one has
so big a house
that he does not need
a good neighbor.

When two do the same,
it is not always the same.

Everyone's friend
      is often
            everyone's fool.

The house that is built
      with every man's advice
      rarely gets a roof.

He who has
      a little money has
            a lot of friends.

One should go invited to
      a friend's house
            in good fortune,
      and uninvited
            in misfortune.

The comforter's head
never aches.

Guests should not forget
to go home.

No one has peace
longer than
his neighbor wishes.

It is never too far
to a friend's house.

One must learn to
make others happy
if one wants
to be happy.

GÅRDAR I LEKSANDS SOCKEN

We should remember
    to think well
        and speak well
            of one another.

Exchange of gifts
    makes friendship
            last.

Home and Family

FINNSTUGAN · VID · STÅNGFALL

Being away
is fine,
being home
is best.

The child acts
in the village
as he has learned
at home.

Late to church,
early to the mill,
this is the way
one returns home sooner.

The pine cone does not fall
far from the tree.

Do not brag of
your father's reputation,
what you have is your own.

Water is thinner than blood.

VID·STÅNGE·HUFVUD·LYSEKIL·

The child puts finery
in her mouth,
the young woman puts it on,
and the old woman keeps it
in her wooden chest.

Honor the house in
which you were born,
the tree that
gave you shade,
and the village where
you were raised.

All little girls are good,
    so where do the
        naughty old women
            come from?

A woman's heart
    sees more than
ten men's eyes.

The stony earth
    grows the corn,
but the woman
      does the work.

Remain a child so that
    your children may
      always love you.

Small children, small worries;
big children, big worries.

A child is
a certain worry and
an uncertain joy.

The motherless child
is in the way when
the stepmother bakes.

ood and Drink

· STRÅKENS · NORDLIGASTE · ÄNDE ·

The sweetest wine
makes the
sharpest vinegar.

Eaten bread
is soon forgotten.

He who has burnt himself once
blows on his soup.

Hunger is the
best seasoning.

One cannot
make soup
out of beauty.

Do not cross the river
to find water.

That which is eaten
from the pot
never comes to
the platter.

The stomach teaches
the hunter to shoot.

When the stomach is satisfied,
the food is bitter.

Every cake
seeks its match.

Where wine
goes in,
wit goes out.

Rural Wisdom

The rich
     have money,
the poor
     have children.

If you want the kernel
     you must crush the nut.

Many mouths make
        an empty dish.

The world's reward
        is ingratitude.

The rich man has five senses,
    the poor man has six.

The poor are not
    those who
        have little,
but those who
        need much.

Poverty does not
        abide stealing,
    and wealth does not
    forbid it.

·KUNGSHALL·KARLSKRONA·

Don't shout before
     you are across
         the stream.

To read and
    not know
  is to plow
    and not sow.

Good will draws
    the load to the village.

A wound never
heals enough
to hide a scar.

He is not rich
who has not
anything old.

Hope keeps the poor alive.
Fear often kills the rich.

Better to bow
than hit your head
on the door lintel.

outh and Old Age

With a young lawyer,
    you lose your inheritance,
  with a young doctor
    you lose your health.

Take hold of grace,
  for younger
    you will never be.

As the young sing,
so the old chirp.

The young do not know
what age is,
and the old forget
what youth was.

Age does not
grant wisdom,
it only makes one
go more slowly.

Being young
is a fault which
improves daily.

The mind of
the young is
like water in
a bucket,
it splashes out
from all sides.

Age's virtues are
dearly purchased.

The young man shows
what the old man was.

He who does not
commit follies
in youth
commits them
in old age.

ife and Death

He who fears death
has lost his zest for life.

Better a
good death
than an evil life.

What life gives,
 death takes.

Death is
 the final doctor.

He who did not
escape from birth
cannot escape
from death.

Death helps us out
 of difficulties,
 but the price is high.

There is no medicine
against death.

Death is
the Lord's broom.

Advice
should not be
viewed from in front,
but from behind.